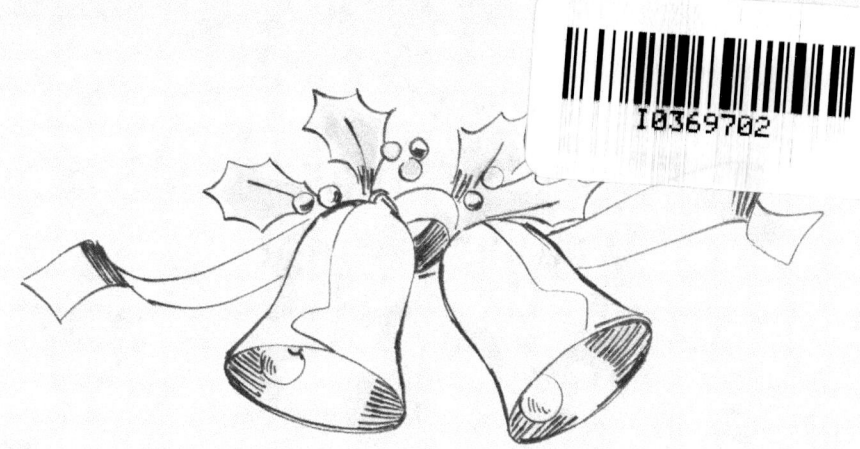

Funny Christmas Creative Writing Prompts

FROM:

TO:

50 Funny Christmas Creative Writing Prompts

Welcome to the festive world of creativity and laughter! In this eBook, we present you with a delightful collection of "50 Funny Christmas Creative Writing Prompts." Embrace the holiday spirit and let your imagination run wild as you explore these humorous scenarios set in the heartwarming backdrop of Christmas.

The holiday season is not only a time for celebration but also an opportunity to indulge in the joy of storytelling. Whether you're an aspiring writer looking for inspiration or simply someone who enjoys the magic of Christmas, these prompts are tailored to tickle your funny bone and ignite your creative spark.

Inside these pages, you'll encounter mischievous elves, talking snowmen, rebellious reindeer, and a myriad of other delightful characters, all caught up in hilarious and unexpected situations. From the whimsical to the absurd, these prompts are designed to challenge your imagination and evoke laughter, making your writing journey both entertaining and enriching.

Feel free to use these prompts as a springboard for your short stories, essays, or even as writing exercises to warm up your creativity during the holiday season. Whether you prefer heartwarming tales of holiday mischief or imaginative adventures in a winter wonderland, these prompts offer a wide range of possibilities, ensuring there's something for every writer to enjoy.

So, grab a cup of hot cocoa, cozy up by the fireplace, and embark on a literary adventure filled with laughter and festive cheer. Let the creativity flow, and may your holiday writing be merry and bright! Happy writing!

How To Use

Here's a guide to help you make the most out of this eBook and spark your creativity during the holiday season.

1. **Explore the Prompts:**
   - Dive into the collection of 50 funny Christmas creative writing prompts. Read through each one to find the ideas that resonate with you the most.
2. **Choose Your Favorites:**
   - Select the prompts that inspire you or make you laugh. You don't have to use them in any particular order – feel free to jump around and let your creativity flow.
3. **Set the Scene:**
   - Consider the characters, settings, and emotions associated with the prompt. Imagine the world in which your story takes place. Is it in a bustling North Pole workshop, a cozy family home, or a magical winter forest?
4. **Develop Your Characters:**
   - Think about who your characters are, their personalities, quirks, and motivations. Give them life by exploring their backgrounds and relationships.
5. **Build the Plot:**
   - Develop the story arc. What challenges will your characters face? How will they overcome obstacles? Will there be unexpected twists and turns? Create a compelling narrative that keeps your readers engaged.
6. **Let Your Creativity Flow:**
   - Don't be afraid to add your unique touch to the prompts. Feel free to modify, combine, or even create entirely new scenarios based on the initial ideas. Your creativity knows no bounds!
7. **Write Freely:**
   - Write without worrying about perfection in your first draft. Let your ideas flow freely and allow your imagination to take you on an adventure. You can always edit and refine later.
8. **Share Your Work:**
   - If you're comfortable, share your creations with others. Whether it's with friends, writing communities, or online platforms, sharing your work can provide valuable feedback and encouragement.
9. **Revisit and Revise:**
   - Revisit your stories after some time has passed. Revise, edit, and polish your work. Sometimes, fresh perspectives can lead to valuable improvements.
10. **Have Fun:**
    - Most importantly, have fun! Writing should be an enjoyable and fulfilling experience. Embrace the humor and joy of the holiday season as you bring these prompts to life.

Now that you know how to use this eBook, it's time to embark on your creative journey.

May your writing be filled with laughter, imagination, and the magic of Christmas! Happy writing!

Santa discovers he's allergic to milk and cookies.

The reindeer unionizes and demands better working conditions.

A mischievous elf invents a new toy that causes chaos at the North Pole.

Rudolph decides to retire and pursue a career in stand-up comedy.

Mrs. Claus accidentally creates a clone of Santa.

Ho ho ho!

The Grinch attends therapy sessions to cope with his holiday issues.

A snowman magically comes to life and becomes a famous pop star.

Santa's sleigh gets a flat tire on Christmas Eve.

The elves go on strike, and chaos ensues in Santa's workshop.

A child writes a letter to Santa asking for the most absurd gift imaginable.

Dear Santa

A family of penguins decides to spend Christmas in the tropics.

Santa's naughty and nice list gets mixed up, leading to unexpected gifts.

A talking Christmas tree gives decorating advice to its owners.

The gingerbread man leads a rebellion against the other holiday treats.

A group of carolers gets trapped in a snowstorm and forms a band.

A snowball fight escalates into an epic battle between neighborhoods.

SNOWball Fight!!

Snowball Fight!!

The Christmas lights in a town come to life and start telling stories.

Santa's reindeer get food poisoning, and chaos erupts on Christmas Eve.

An alien visits Earth on Christmas and gets confused by holiday traditions.

A group of kids decides to catch Santa in the act on Christmas Eve.

ho! ho! ho!

The Christmas presents rebel against being wrapped and demand freedom.

A talking snow globe grants wishes but with unintended consequences.

Santa's elves accidentally shrink themselves and embark on an adventure.

The North Pole gets a tropical heatwave, causing Christmas chaos.

A cat and a dog team up to save Christmas from a mischievous raccoon.

A snowman starts melting but discovers he has magical powers.

Santa's sleigh gets upgraded with high-tech gadgets, leading to hilarious mishaps.

A Christmas tree with a sense of humor plays pranks on the family.

The ghost of Christmas past decides to take a vacation.

A group of holiday characters (Santa, the Easter Bunny, etc.) form a rock band.

Santa's elves create a social media platform for magical creatures.

The Christmas turkey escapes and embarks on a journey to avoid being eaten.

A talking candy cane helps a child navigate the challenges of the holiday season.

Santa's workshop adopts eco-friendly practices, causing humorous complications.

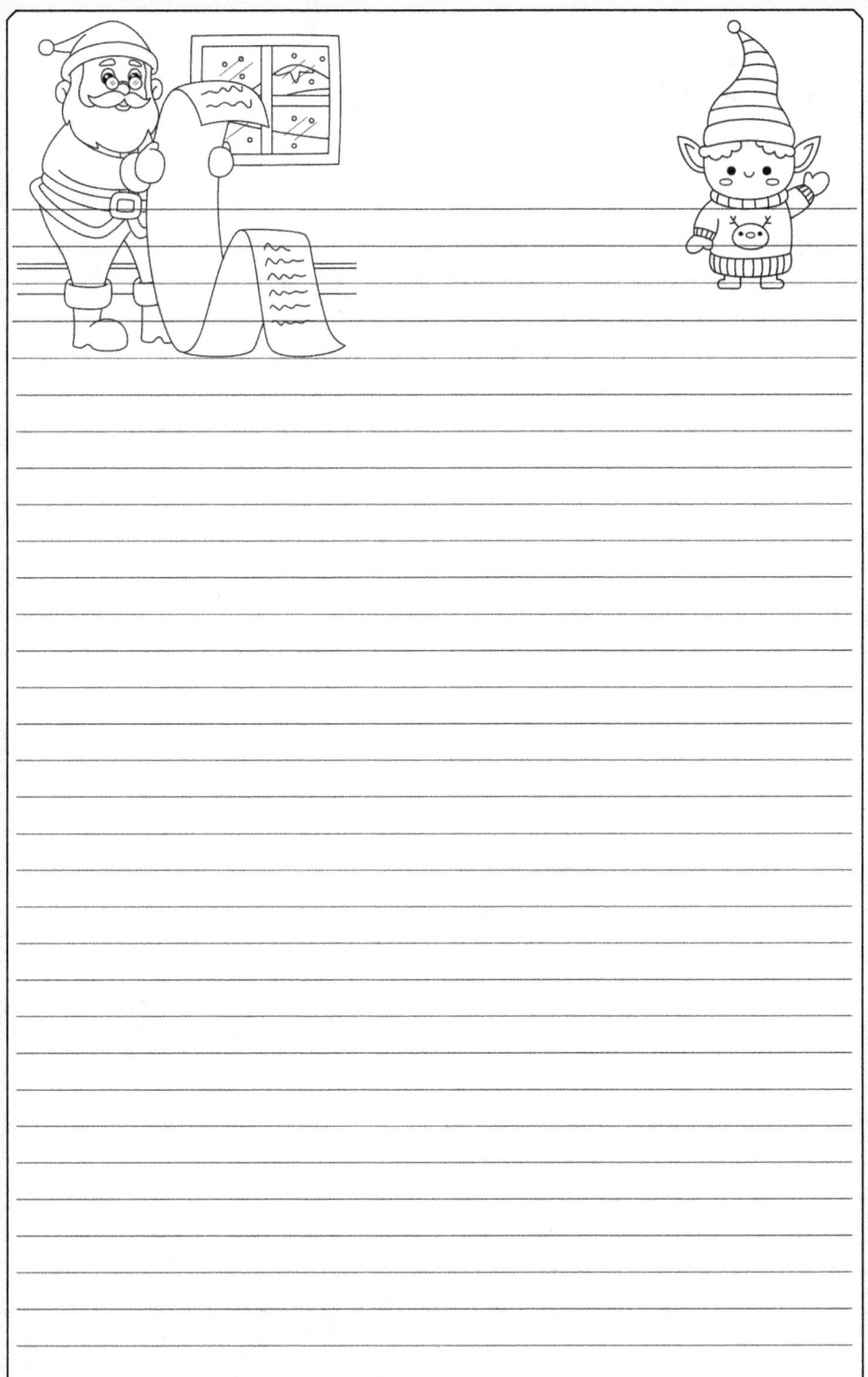

A snowflake dreams of being unique and sets out on a quest to find its special talent.

An ambitious elf tries to take over Santa's workshop with disastrous results.

A family receives a magical ornament that brings their Christmas dinner to life.

Santa's sleigh is powered by something unexpected, like laughter or hugs.

HO
HO
HO

A mischievous elf starts a prank war in the North Pole.

The Christmas decorations come alive at night and throw a wild party.

Santa's elves accidentally create a batch of mischievous toys that wreak havoc.

A child's imaginary friend comes to life and helps them save Christmas.

MERRY Christmas

A Christmas tree salesman discovers his trees can communicate with each other.

Santa's reindeer form a band and enter a talent competition.

snowman and a sandcastle engage in a rivalry over which is better.

A group of talking presents helps a child find the perfect gift for their parents.

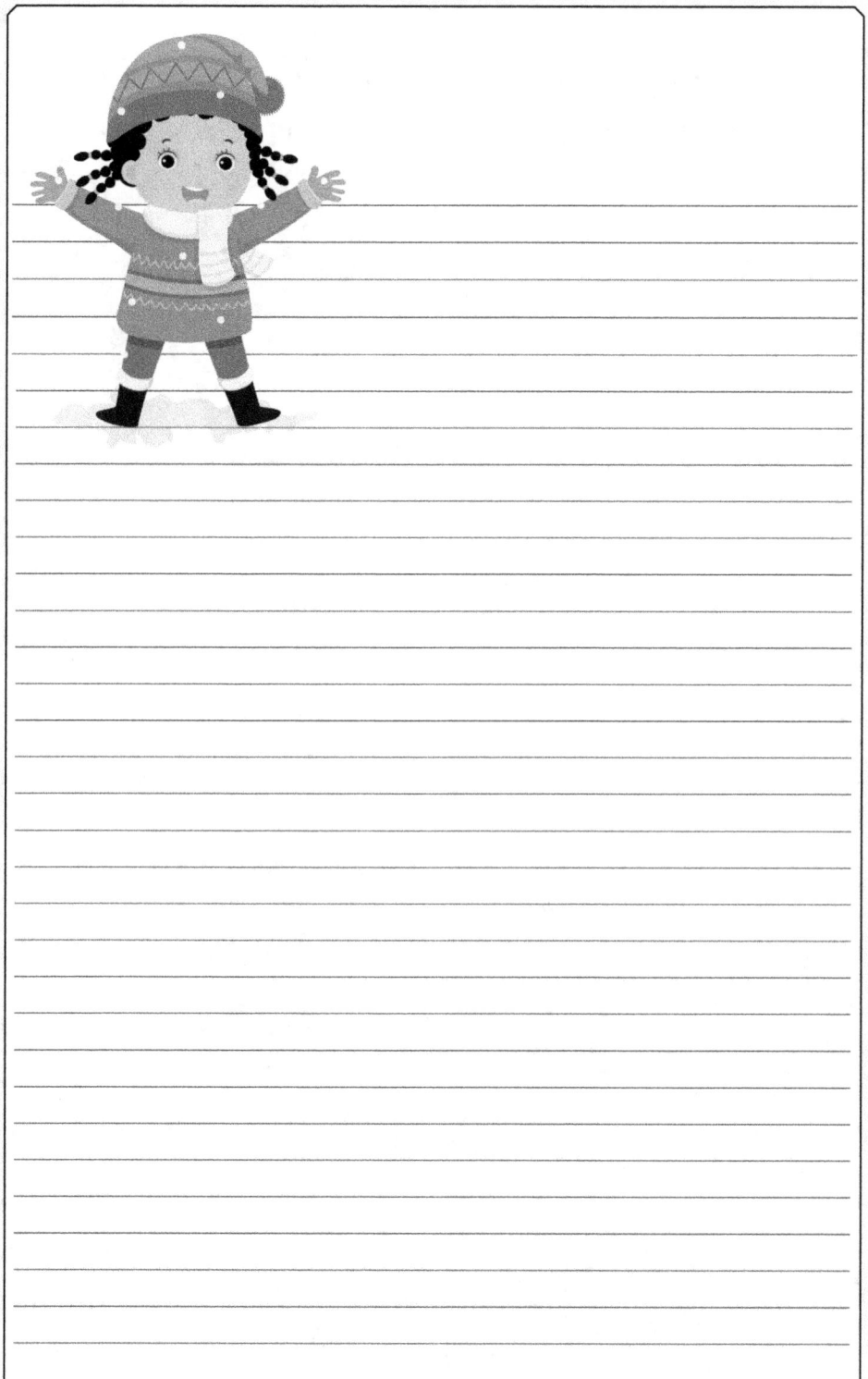

An elf invents a device that allows people to experience Christmas in virtual reality.

A town's Christmas lights competition gets out of control as neighbors compete.

Santa's sleigh is accidentally teleported to a different country, causing confusion.

ho! ho! ho!

A group of Christmas characters attends therapy sessions to deal with holiday stress.

www.ingramcontent.com/pod-product-compliance
Lightning Source LLC
Chambersburg PA
CBHW071010080526
44587CB00015B/2412